This special book belongs to

_____

_____

_____

Copyright © Anna Cerridwen 2024

Published with Ingram Spark

First published 2024

ISBN: 978 106832761 2

All rights reserved. No part of this publication may be reproduced, stored in a retrieval system, or transmitted, in any form or by any means, electronic, mechanical, photocopying, recording or otherwise, without the prior permission of the publishers.

# My bonus dad is the best

Written by Anna Cerridwen

Illustrated by Natasha Poposka - de Bats

I love my bonus dad;
he's good to me.

He makes me smile,
I'm happy as can be.

My bonus dad loves me
and will always be there.

He gives hugs if I want them,
and oodles of care.

My bonus dad can't fly;
he has no magic powers,

But I would pick him,
if bonus dads were flowers.

He likes to play games,
to be silly and funny,

We kick balls outside
when it's nice and sunny.

If I fall, he puts a plaster on my knee.

He's patient and kind and loving to me.

He makes me laugh,
he jokes and he sings.

My bonus dad teaches me
loads of new things.

He teaches me it
doesn't matter who won,

What's important is
to have lots of fun.

He gently brushes
my hair with a comb,

He brings lots of happiness
into our home.

He cooks yummy meals
and he washes my clothes,

Never shouts at me,
even when I'd hurt his nose!

We sit down together
and read lots of books.

When in the kitchen,
we pretend to be cooks.

We have so much fun
when we visit the park,

Sometimes we pretend
he's a big, scary shark!

By the end of the day
when I am all mucky,

He runs me a bath
and I feel very lucky.

My bonus dad is great,
the best I could wish for.

Someone who cares,
and who I adore.

I don't mind if he earns hundreds of dollar bucks,

Whether he cycles, rides horses or drives big trucks.

He could look nothing like me,
be tall or small,

What he looks like
doesn't matter at all.

All that's important is
he really loves me.

I've got the best bonus dad
there ever could be!